# Yellowknife

*Photography: HANS O. BARFOD*
*Text: Carolyn Czarnecki*

Outcrop Ltd.
Yellowknife, Northwest Territories

First Printing 1981
Second Printing 1984

Outcrop Ltd.
ISBN 0-919315-02-X

Additional Photographs:
Alex Czarnecki (pg. 13t), Carolyn Czarnecki (pg. 49b), Ronne
Hemming (pg. 32, 38), Mike Hewitt (pg. 28/29, 36, 49t, 57t, 58),
Rodd Raycroft (pg. 37), Brian Thompson (pg. 6/7, 30, 31)

Outcrop Ltd.
The Northern Publishers
Box 1350
Yellowknife, N.W.T., Canada, X1A 2N9
Printed and bound in Canada

# Yellowknife

*Photography: HANS O. BARFOD*
*Text: Carolyn Czarnecki*

## Hans Barfod

Hans Barfod was born in Denmark and lived in Greenland for two years before coming to Canada in 1957. An architect, Hans lived and worked in Montreal for 10 years....three years as a designer at Expo 67. He first moved north in 1967 and finally settled in Yellowknife in 1969.

A graduate of the Royal Academy of Fine Arts, Copenhagen, Hans is an accomplished artist and musician as well as a photographer. His photographs have appeared in the Canadian Geographic magazine as well as other publications, and his paintings have been shown in Vancouver galleries.

In his work with the Government of the N.W.T. Hans has travelled extensively in the Canadian Arctic.

## Carolyn Pogue Czarnecki

Carolyn migrated to the NWT in 1970 and calls Yellowknife Home.

Since arriving, she has worked as librarian, craft teacher, researcher, editor and properties chief for many stage productions.

At present she is writing and reading poetry to groups of children, polishing a 3 act play, writing the script for a film about Yellowknife and working as secretary at Mildred Hall Elementary School. In her spare time she works in the Peace Movement and tries to maintain a clear path between her front door and the typewriter in her home on Latham Island.

Carolyn and her husband Alex live with 3 other Czarneckis: Michael, Andrea and Kathryn.

Yellowknife . . . Canada's newest capital city . . . a city founded on permafrost, muskeg and the ancient rock of the Canadian Shield, a city built on dreams, perseverance and the ingenuity of a daring group of pioneers, who braved the long, harsh winters and 24 hours of summer sunshine in tents.

Nine hundred and sixty-five air kilometres north of Edmonton, and 442 kilometres south of the Arctic Circle, Yellowknife hugs the north shore of Great Slave Lake.

Yellowknife . . . home, now, to 10,000 people, one-quarter of the population of Canada's vast Northwest Territories.

Yellowknife . . . a city of piquant contrasts. In December, children leave for school in the dead of night. They will see the sun rise at morning recess, eat lunch in the full light of day, and watch the sun set again before going home under the Northern Lights. In June, their parents begin a game of golf under the midnight sun.

Yellowknife . . . where one woman scrapes a caribou hide at home in the traditional way, while her neighbour writes computer programs in a nearby Government office . . . where one man hauls in a day's catch of whitefish to be smoked and dried at home for the winter's meals, while another conducts his business in an air-conditioned conference room of a local hotel.

To the surprise of many first-time visitors, Yellowknife doesn't, at first glance, look much different from any small, modern city in southern Canada. No igloos or teepees line the main street. But a closer look reveals that Yellowknife is a city with a difference.

What could be more distinctive than a house that was skidded into Yellowknife on a winter ice road from an old mine at Giauque Lake, or another, trucked up

the gravel highway from a pre-fab factory in Calgary, Alberta, and other houses built by the pioneers of the '30s, from timber that grew where the city centre now stands?

And the people who live in these homes are as varied as the wild flowers on the tundra. Some, like the flowers, are native to the country; the Dogrib tribe of the Dene (pronouned De-nay) Nation still reside here along with members of other tribes. Newer residents came from all parts of Canada, from India, Europe, Britain, the United States, the Phillipines — from all over the world. This makes Yellowknife a fascinating melting pot of cultures, a cosmopolitan city.

It is a small city, as cities go, but a complete one.

There are shopping centres, special education programs in modern schools, recreation facilities and air transportation to the world *Outside*. Films, radio, television . . . it's all here. With it is a small town friendliness, a caring and sharing.

Welcome to Yellowknife. It's a special corner of the world.

# History in brief

It may seem like an unlikely spot for a city. Yet, for countless generations, people lived and made their living in the Yellowknife area. Detah, across Yellowknife Bay, was a favorite camping place for the Dene. The lakes nearby yielded bountiful catches of whitefish, pickerel, grayling, trout and pike, and the skies echoed to the cries of migrating duck and geese in the fall. Game was plentiful. Herds of caribou would be intercepted in their yearly migrations, and followed far to the north from the easy access given at the mouth of the Yellowknife River.

Then the explorers came. Samuel Hearne in his quest for better trading routes and more furs pushed north to Great Slave Lake as early as the 1700s. By 1789, a trading post had been established near the mouth of Yellowknife Bay. Here the Yellowknife Dene, named for their copper weapons and utensils, came to trade.

In the late 1890s, prospectors passed through the area on their way to the Yukon gold fields. Some stopped; and, at the mouth of the Yellowknife River, one found gold.

But the task of opening a hard rock mine on the north shore of Great Slave was no simple matter and the area was left to nature and the Dene for another 35 years. Stories of gold at Yellowknife faded to mere rumours.

The rumours remained whispers until the 1930s when technology caught up to the North. The drone of tiny aircraft was heard in Northern skies. The "work-horse of the North" was beginning its career. Planes brought mail, medicine and prospectors, many of them jobless men desperate for a dream.

Pitchblende, containing radium, was discovered at Great Bear Lake in 1931, following oil strikes at Norman Wells. Then gold was rediscovered at Yellow-knife, and when its presence was con-firmed by Dr. A. W. Jolliffe of the Geo-logical Survey of Canada in 1935, the news was accidentally leaked, and . . .

*Boom!* Men left dustbowl farms and de-pression wracked cities, packed a year's supply of food, some prospecting tools and headed for Yellowknife. By barge, scow and floatplane they came. Women followed. Few struck it rich. But hund-reds of claims were staked, and two mines, Negus and the Con went into pro-duction. The first gold brick was poured at the Con in 1938. By 1940 work had started on seven minesites.

Yellowknife camp was an exciting place to be. Planes bringing new settlers and supplies buzzed in from Edmonton five times a week. A sternwheeler plied the lake, replaced in winter by cat-trains from Fort Resolution on the Slave River route.

The first home for many a miner was a tent on a frame floor. But gradually tents were replaced by shacks. Rough-log hotels and cafes served a rapidly expand-ing clientele. The first schoolteacher, Mildred Hall, was hired in 1939. The Con hired Dr. Ollie Stanton, the first doctor, who went on to deliver most of the com-munity's babies. A village was born.

The early '40s were years of despair for Yellowknife, for Canada, for the world. Men left for war. Helmet replaced hardhat. Mines closed or slowed down. Yellowknife waited.

But when the fighting was done the boom was on again. Yellowknife's popu-lation increased dramatically. The original townsite, Old Town and Latham Island, was bursting at the seams. There was nowhere to go but up . . . up the hill to New Town. By the late '40s, construc-tion had begun on several new buildings in New Town, where the city centre is now located. For residents up the hill, outdoor toilets, honey buckets and water buckets were things of the past.

By 1950 Yellowknife boasted a landing strip for wheeled aircraft at Long Lake, a seven-member Board of Trustees re-sponsible for municipal affairs (three of these were elected and four were ap-pointed by Ottawa), a new Red Cross Hospital on Frame Lake, and a golf course.

A causeway named after Yellowknife's first newspaperman, big, whiskey-drink-ing Jock McMeekan joined Latham Island to the mainland. CFYK, a volunteer-run radio station began broadcasting in 1950. In 1953 Yellowknifers went to the polls and elected their first mayor, J. G. McNiven. Yellowknife was growing up!

Bush Pilots' Monument atop the "Rock" in Old Town.

Planes of every make and vintage line the float plane wharves in Old Town.

Downtown Yellowknife today...just up the hill from the float plane base.

In 1961, the final section of an all-weather gravel road was completed and Yellowknife's links with the *Outside* were strengthened. Now, big trucks loaded with fresh produce and the latest appliances made their way North. Tourists began to appear, and residents could motor out for vacations or business. The road did much to reduce Yellowknife's reliance on aircraft. But even today, Yellowknifers rely on the airplane during freeze-up and break-up, when the Fort Providence ferry and the ice road across the Mackenzie River are out of service.

Yellowknife's transformation from a small, remote mining camp into the modern urban centre it is today began in 1967. In that year, Stuart M. Hodgson was appointed the Northwest Territories' first resident Commissioner, and the Government of the Northwest Territories moved lock, stock and barrel from Ottawa to the NWT's newly-named capital — Yellowknife. Houses went up in a hurry, as construction companies scurried to meet the needs of the newcomers. Businesses grew, and more sophisticated services became available. Northern Region Headquarters for the Department of National Defence moved to Yellowknife, continuing the housing boom.

In 1970 came the crowning touch: Yellowknife became a City. It is the first, and to date, the only city in Canada's enormous Northwest Territories. To the visitor standing in the wilderness just outside Yellowknife, it may seem an unlikely spot for a city. But here it is! Canada's most northerly city.

# On the rocks

**A**s Yellowknifers go about their daily business, they walk on ground laden with a metal that has, through the ages, driven men wild. *Where the gold is paved with streets,* wrote Robin Beaumont in an original Yellowknife musical.

The Canadian Shield is an oasis of wonder and discovery for the detectives of the Rock Set. Scheelite, amethyst, spodumene, beryl, and the odd bit of gold-flecked quartz await the strike of the prospector's hammer. Enthusiasts spend hours under the midnight sun, hiking over outcroppings and through muskeg, swatting mosquitos and filling their sample bags.

Showings at Burwash Point on the east side of Yellowknife Bay brought the deluge of gold seekers in, and although a mine was never developed there, ore-hungry men soon had most of the western shoreline staked. Three mines have produced gold (and a little silver) within the city.

Murdoch Mosher first staked Cominco property in 1934, and 14 claims were soon in place alongside his staked by Cominco employees Russell, McCrea and Finland after the company received a hot tip. They staked in the late fall with the snow gently falling on their shoulders, not knowing if they were staking worthless rock or Aladdin's treasure.

Mosher was told by two experts that his claims were worthless and he left the North. Had he been in the camp at the time, however, he might not have heed-

Remnants of early mines are overshadowed by Con Mine's new Robertson Shaft.

ed the bad advice. Tom Payne, a prospector and mechanic, had one eye on Mosher's claims, and the other on the clock as the lapse time neared. On August 22, 1936, at the stroke of midnight, Payne and his friend Gordon Latham drove new posts into the ground. When they finished, they saw that they had been only minutes ahead of roughly 30 men who had the same idea. Payne and his backers sold out to Cominco for half a million dollars and 40% interest in the property.

Cominco poured the first gold brick in the Northwest Territories on September 5, 1938. Forty years later, the mile-deep Robertson shaft was completed on the same property. A towering landmark, this shaft allows more exploration, development and production of gold from lower levels of the mine. Murdoch Mosher missed a fortune.

Negus Mine, south of Cominco, was originally staked by Ollie Hagen and Lockie Burwash in 1936. Only 3 years later they poured their first gold brick. For a brief time during the war, Cominco ceased production, and Negus remained the only mine pouring the glittering metal. It had to stop for a few months, however, in 1944, when the war in Europe made domestic gold production too costly. It began production again in 1945, and continued until final closure in 1952.

On the north side of the camp, C. J. Baker and H. Muir were sent in to find ore for Giant Yellowknife Gold Mines Ltd. The mining recorder's office logged their claims in 1935. In 1948 the first brick was poured, and the underground mine and open pits of Giant Yellowknife have been part of the Yellowknife scene ever since.

15

Max Ward's Bristol Freighter,
the first wheeled aircraft to land
at the North Pole, stands at the
entrance to the city.

# On the wing

**B**ush flying was almost born in the North. It's certainly here that the light airplane came into its own during the '30s. It is doubtful that Yellowknife would have been established without those mechanical birds. Two landmarks in the city honour the brave pilots who flew and fly them. They symbolize the North's dependency on, and love affair with the planes.

The Bristol aircraft at the entrance to the city, in 1967 was the first wheeled aircraft to land at the North Pole. It was retired from service in 1968 and donated by Max Ward of Wardair to the city. It now sits majestically overlooking Long Lake, a short distance from the airport.

The Bush Pilot's Monument is a sleek, stainless steel figure atop a stone cairn. It is situated on *The Rock*, the highest point in the Old Town and a landmark for generations of pilots.

Throughout Yellowknife's short life, the buzz of bush planes has meant news and new faces. Prospectors, geologists, hunters, tourists, officials and royalty have all been on the wing coming and going to the capital. Now, the buzz is joined by the roar of jets and a cluttering of helicopters.

On wheels, skis, or pontoons, at the airport or in Old Town, Yellowknife is a flying buff's paradise.

At times one of the busiest airports in Canada, Yellowknife is living proof that man was meant to fly, and the little "workhorse of the North" to carry him.

# Who are we?

The Great Slave Lake area has been inhabited by nomadic peoples from time immemorial. The Dene were harvesters of the lakes and the land. When fur traders, and later mining men came north, the old ways began to change. Settlements took root. But although Yellowknife owes its beginnings to the minerals beneath it, many residents still hunt, fish and trap. Here a trapper and a businessman may live side by side, and both are content; each gives to and takes from the other's world.

Gold started this town, and gold has helped to keep it alive. More than six hundred miners work the shifts at Giant Yellowknife and Con mines. Some are colourful old-timers who remember the pioneer days in Yellowknife; others are new northerners working to make a life for their families in a new country.

Government occupies by far the largest proportion of Yellowknife's population. Municipal, territorial and federal employees follow an almost bewildering variety of professions and trades in the City — everything from pounding a typewriter to pounding the beat. Canada's historic Royal Canadian Mounted Police maintain a Regional Headquarters at Yellowknife. Teachers are employed by seven schools, from kindergarten to grade 12.

Yellowknife, from its earliest days, has always had a thriving business community. Today's Yellowknife businesses supply everything from art to contract drilling, from safety boots to gourmet meals.

Many Yellowknife residents have been attracted from *Outside*. Some are transferred here for a brief tour of duty; others hanker for big city living or a warmer climate after a while. But some were born here, and there are also many who come for a year and stay for a lifetime. One well-known lady came to visit her sister for two months . . . 39 years ago!

18

# Where
# we live

The original log or frame buildings of Yellowknife's pioneer days linger on in the Old Town and at the two minesites. But brand new owner-designed homes constantly take root in the subdivisions and are sprinkled throughout the older areas.

Many Yellowknife homes are marvels of patchwork and ingenuity. Permafrost, or blue ice is sometimes only a few metres from the surface, so building a house here can be difficult. Sometimes piles must be sunk to bedrock level before a house can safely sit on its lot. Some houses have literally been pinned to the rock and others sit on thick insulating pads of gravel, disguised by a suburban lawn.

Adventurous people who admire the view of the lake have built atop the rocks in Old Town like the first residents, and struggle with bags of groceries up long flights of stairs as a consequence. Some houses try to follow the shape of the lot, occasionally at precarious angles; some content themselves with blending into the natural surroundings with stained wood or log exteriors.

At the north end of Latham Island is Rainbow Valley, so named because the first string of houses there was painted an impressive spectrum of bright colours in honour of a Royal visit some years ago. Here, the community centre too is decorated with a spirited rainbow.

The Valley's Dene inhabitants have chosen a distinctive traditional lifestyle.

21

There is a community kindergarten, run in Dogrib and English by the Tree of Peace Friendship Centre and there is a colourful confusion of boats and dogs, smokehouses and skidoos.

The Old Town waterfront is always a lively place. Small planes buzz in and out, landing on floats in summer and skis in winter. Graceful sailboats compete with canoes and motorboats for space in the Bay as soon as the lake ice moves out. Sometimes a barge moored at the Government dock looms out of the morning mist like a ghostly castle. People drive, skidoo, ski, snowshoe or mush their dogs across the ice in winter. Warehouses and homes dot the area's distinguishing landmark, the Old Town *Rock*, and a fine view of the bustling panorama of activity may be had from the Bush Pilot's Monument at its summit.

Peace River and Willow Flats are located on either side of Franklin Avenue just past the *Rock*, at the bottom of the hill leading to New Town. Pioneers settled here, close to the water's edge.

Today, the Flats are home to Yellowknifers who prefer a less conforming, more relaxed environment and way of life. Along the unpaved, narrow streets, renovated and new houses, often of unusual design and whimsical appearance, rub shoulders with Quonset huts, converted buses, log cabins, one-room shanties and the original settlers' clapboard homes. Yards are filled with a bewildering array of things that "might come in handy, some day." Part of the area's unique charm is its residents' willingness to lend a hand, a tool or a spare piece of scrap lumber to a neighbour in need.

The School Draw area, south of the Flats, was one of Yellowknife's first subdivisions. The walls of the draw are solid rock, and its floor is mostly muskeg. It is no small feat of engineering and stubbornness that homes are here at all —

several residents experienced a sinking feeling in the pit of the stomach that was more than psychological, as expensive houses heaved, buckled and sank into the permafrost. Ingenuity and persistence paid off in attractive modern homes, some with a view of Great Slave Lake.

Up the hill, in the best small-town tradition, the Post Office and a local coffee-shop are the focal "people places" of Yellowknife's downtown core. Here the visitor has a chance to see and meet just about everybody in town — civil servants at a breakfast meeting, politicians chatting with constituents, trappers just in from the bush with their families, miners discussing the latest metal prices posted on the board. Nestled alongside office buildings the signs of the first building boom are still evident. Tidy frame homes with neat gardens are a fine example of the late '60s and shoulder to shoulder march rows of apartments and townhouses, built to house the burgeoning ranks of Government.

Yellowknife's new City Hall sits on the shore of Frame Lake. Visitors with a proclamation to make will find this building's exterior staircase the ideal place! With luck, the City Band or the pipers might turn out. Many Yellowknife events do, in fact, begin from the steps of City Hall, or take place nearby in the Gerry Murphy Arena or the Prince of Wales Northern Heritage Centre. Winter or summer, the Heritage Centre's artistic and historical exhibits, set in a spacious interior of natural wood, filled with sunshine, provide refreshment for the spirit.

During the '70s, houses seemed to spring up like mushrooms after a rain. The south end of Franklin Avenue past 54th street saw rapid development as land was taken from the wilderness for homes. Farther on, past the hospital, Northland Trailer Park was set up, and still further from its beginning, two more

new subdivisions round out the Yellow-knife plan.

Much of Yellowknife is a walker's city. From one end of Franklin Avenue to the other, from the Old Town to the newest of the new, the City stretches only 6.5 kilometres. Anywhere along the route, the casual pedestrian is liable to find interesting and sometimes amusing sights. A glance into a downtown backyard might produce a return glare from a billygoat or a fine crop of potatoes. Yellowknife has a flourishing contingent of urban farmers. A small building announces imperial ambitions with the grand title of *The Roman Empire Building*!

Flanking Yellowknife, the Giant and Con minesites round out the citys' form. Con's new Robertson headframe, with its bold orange crown, is a prominent Yellowknife landmark to the southeast. Across the great vein of gold-bearing rock that underlies the City, the pleasant frame buildings of Giant Yellowknife Mines cluster to the northwest on Back Bay.

Fewer people now live at the minesites than in Yellowknife's early days, but the feel of close-knit and functional communities still remains. Utilidors, surface water, heat and sewer lines, zig-zag over the rocks. They were insulated in the beginning with moss and boxed in with lumber. Most of the original frame buildings from the '30s and '40s have stood well, weathering in harmony with their surroundings. Lean, honest, hardworking, they personify the pioneers whose initiative and daring made Yellowknife possible.

23

# Building?
# Which
# building?

It's the age of conservation, and Canadians are always hearing about the value of recycling used articles. "Recycle your paper, recycle your bottles, recycle your tin cans!" the harrassed householder is told. Yellowknife is light-years ahead of all this. It has been for decades. Yellowknifers recycle their buildings!

Yellowknife's dry climate is kind to wooden structures. That fact, combined with the high cost of construction materials, encourages a chameleon-like existence for many buildings. Not to mention some confusing directions to newcomers.

"Where's a craft shop?" asks a tourist. A typical reply is often "It's in the old Northern Health Building," or "It's across from the old liquor store." It's not unusual to find buildings several times relocated or adapted to new purposes.

The old Rex Cafe, which in the late '60s looked as if it just couldn't decide in which direction to collapse, was moved from its prominent waterfront location on Latham Island to the bottom of School Draw. It was restored and painted a bright yellow and became the home of Yellowknife's second weekly newspaper. In 1979 it was repainted a dignified brown.

When the Pentecostal church grew into bigger facilities, the tiny log chapel became a residence.

The shoemaker's house briefly became a lawyer's office. When the site was needed for a telephone exchange, the house was moved and later became, reasonably enough, a secondhand shop.

One fine summer evening hydro workers were seen raising lines and measuring things along the length of Franklin Avenue between the Old Town and the city centre. These mysterious actions paved the way for moving one of the larger uptown buildings: the theatre. The old *Capitol* moved majestically down the hill, coming to rest at the water's edge. There it received a facelift and it too began a new life.

The original Pentecostal chapel...now a home for Old Town residents.

There is another Yellowknife survival story of note. It concerns a very old commercial building that for once serves its original purpose on its original site. This is Old Town's Wildcat Cafe, first opened by Willie Wylie and Smokey Stout in 1937. This log building was for years a place where people gathered for meals, a cup of coffee and friendly conversation. When activity moved up the hill, it was used for a warehouse, and later was abandoned to other patrons: hornets, bees, birds and mice. It began to disintegrate. In the late '70s a loosely-knit group of volunteers, The Old Stope Association, undertook the difficult task of saving the Wildcat. It took three years, and today visitors can once more enjoy the relaxed atmosphere, a view of the float bases, and old-fashioned home-cooked meals at the Wildcat.

Overlooking the Wildcat, a forlorn boiler sits amid a barely traceable concrete foundation. This was the site of not one, but two buildings which shunned being recycled. The Old Stope, in 1949 and then the Yellowknife Hotel in 1968, burned to the ground taking with them a host of memories of Yellowknife's good old days.

# What on earth do you do up there?

Spectacular displays of Northern Lights announce the beginning of Autumn. It's a time for finding out who grew the city's biggest pumpkin at the Fall Fair; for checking traps in preparation for long days on the trap line; for sitting down to a feast of wild duck a l'orange. Many Yellowknifers sign up for evening classes, or join some of the 100 clubs, associations or leagues. With activities ranging from crafts to dog mushing, from community service to cadets or Ukrainian dancing, Yellowknifers are more likely to complain of exhaustion than boredom.

In the past, drama groups have provided popular entertainment. Yellowknifers have staged operettas, musicals and dramas over the years, one even a homegrown musical, *Two Hands and Forever*, based on the early days in Yellowknife.

Autumn is also a time when the Legislative Assembly begins a new year of sittings, and many residents take advantage of the availability of Legislative meetings to watch members from all over the Territory tackle the administration of this vast area of Canada. The assembly sits in other parts of the Territories on a rotating basis throughout the year.

In winter, some Yellowknifers like to curl up by the hearth with a good book from the local Library. Others resist the urge to hibernate during this season of ice-fogs, sundogs and darkness by participating in winter sports. (The more enthusiastically you participate, the warmer you stay!) Cross-country skiing, skating and hockey, dog mushing, snowshoeing, ice fishing and hunting for caribou, ptarmigan and hare are typical activities. Indoor sports, from racquetball to swimming, also contribute to the glow on winter faces.

In March we celebrate the advent of spring with the *Caribou Carnival*. As carnivals go, it's one of the best. The highlight is the Canadian Championship Dog Derby, a test of endurance by anyone's standards. The race is over 240 kilometres long and takes place over three days. The course extends out over Great Slave Lake. Dog mushers come from all over Canada and the U.S. to compete. Other carnival events include log sawing, broom ball, bingo-on-ice, tea-boiling contests, flour-packing and igloo-building. The festivities are held on Frame Lake, which by then has an ice cover more than a metre thick.

Spring comes quickly, when it arrives. The ice bridge over the Mackenzie River goes out, bedding plants are started indoors, and ducks and students return from the south.

Midsummer activities reach their high point, along with the sun, on June 21. That night is celebrated as *Raven Mad Daze*, and the fun whirls on past midnight. The Midnight Golf Tournament is one such event. Two things make golfing here unique: the ravens and the course itself. One of the hazards of the course is the friendly, cheeky symbol of the city — the raven. The object of his game is to see how many golf balls he can steal. The course is distinctive, the greens are really brown and the entire course is sand. Tee-off time, naturally, is midnight.

The weekend of the 21st is also a treat for the musically-inclined. The annual music festival, *Folk On The Rocks* brings together entertainers from North and South for three days of outdoor concerts and workshops. It's an opportunity for everyone to make a joyful noise!

In the early days, Yellowknife's boating population consisted of the local people catching supper, water taxis offering rides to Latham Island or the minesites, and barges bringing in winter supplies from the south. The barges still come in, and people still go out to catch something for supper, but now the lake is dotted with

dozens and dozens of pleasure craft as well, from sailboats to cabin cruisers. It's a "top of the world" feeling to enjoy a freshly-caught trout around a campfire, and it's a beautiful sight to look out on the bay and see a sail catch the sun around midnight.

With cooler days and longer nights, the seasonal round begins again.

In Yellowknife, as at Alice's Restaurant, you can do anything you want; if it's not here already, you can make it happen. That's the spirit of Yellowknife, past and present.

With 20 hours of daylight plus four hours of dusk, Yellowknifers take full advantage of the short northern summer.

March is a fine time for winter
sports in Yellowknife . . . then
the long hours of daylight in
April herald the northern spring.

Yellowknifers take full advantage
of the short but pleasant
summers.

At the winter solstice,
Yellowknife has less than five
hours of daylight and
temperatures can drop to -40º.

To overcome "cabin fever", Yellowknifers join in the festivities of Caribou Carnival or cheer on their favorite team in the Canadian Championship Dog Derby.

The Prince of Wales Northern Heritage Centre, with its arched roof, displays the history of the North, while the angular Canadian Broadcasting Corporation building is part of the modern face of Yellowknife.

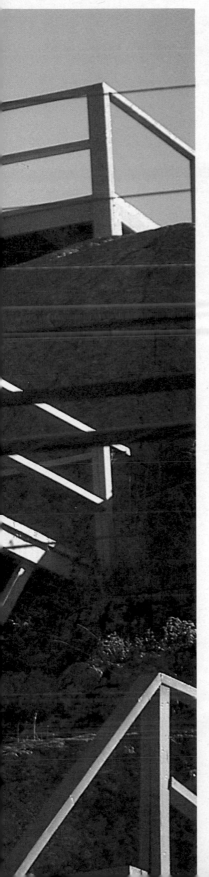

From high atop the rock, to the shores of Great Slave Lake, signs of Yellowknife's past survive.

43

Wild roses, juniper and fireweed...splashes of colour in a rocky landscape.

Yellowknife's sophisticated city
hall....a proud statement of a
city founded on gold.

54

Hand hewn logs are not uncommon among the older buildings of Yellowknife.

On a cold winter day, ice fog
envelops the downtown area.
Residents of Rainbow Valley on
Latham Island combine traditional activities with city living.

This modern log structure is a far cry from its humble ancestor.

On an autumn day in Yellowknife, bleached summer colors change to midnight blue, and like the year, are suddenly gone.

Outcrop Ltd.
Yellowknife, Northwest Territories